"When good Americans die, they go to Paris."

Oscar Wilde

Made in the USA
Las Vegas, NV
09 April 2025

20747478R00056